Heywood Broun

AS HE SEEMED TO US

Heywood Broun

AS HE SEEMED TO US

BY

JOHN L. LEWIS · FRANKLIN P. ADAMS

HERBERT BAYARD SWOPE

FIORELLO H. LaGUARDIA · CARL RANDAU · LEWIS GANNETT

EDNA FERBER · JOHN KIERAN · CHARLES HOROWITZ

KARL VIRAG · MORRIS L. ERNST · QUENTIN REYNOLDS

THEODORE S. KENYON · FRANK SULLIVAN

GARDNER JACKSON · EDWARD G. ROBINSON

KENNETH G. CRAWFORD · A. J. ISSERMAN

EDWARD McNAMARA · FATHER EDWARD DOWLING

ROLLIN KIRBY

Biographical commentaries by

MORRIS WATSON *and* ERNEST L. MEYER

PUBLISHED FOR

THE NEWSPAPER GUILD OF NEW YORK

117 WEST 46TH STREET · NEW YORK, N. Y.

BY RANDOM HOUSE · 1940

THE following pages are a stenographic record of the Heywood Broun Memorial meeting which was held under the auspices of the Newspaper Guild of New York at Manhattan Center, 34th Street and Eighth Avenue, New York, on the evening of February 12, 1940. An invited audience of 12,000 persons attended.

> Norman Lloyd was the narrator of the biographical introductory material written by Morris Watson and Ernest L. Meyer.
> William Schneider announced the speakers.
> Saul Mills was the program director.

The biographical portion of the memorial program was followed by an auction of objets de Broun and autographed volumes donated by famous American authors and inscribed in memory of Heywood Broun. The proceeds will go toward establishment of Heywood Broun Memorial awards for newspapermen.

Clifton Fadiman and Jerome Brooks conducted the auction.

The program ended with the singing of "A Ballad for Americans," words by John LaTouche and music by Earl Robinson, with Alfred Sachs conducting Mr. Robinson's chorus. Jules Bledsoe was the soloist.

Through the memory of his friends and associates, we present the intimate biography of Heywood Broun (1888-1939). He was born in Brooklyn on December 7, 1888, and named Heywood Campbell Broun. He was educated at Horace Mann School, where he was voted best all-around man in his class. At Harvard, in the class with John Reed, Hamilton Fish, Stuart Chase, Walter Lippmann and others, he played basketball, favored study of the Bible as English literature, and failed to make the Crimson or to graduate.

HEYWOOD, the schoolboy, with his shoelace untied, his rumpled hair and his kindly, twinkling eyes, his clumsy gait and drawling speech, looks at us tonight over the peaks and valleys of the intervening years.

Theodore S. Kenyon　　Slow and ungainly, he was heavy enough to hold the line as center on the football team, and tall enough to out-reach his opponents at basketball. Alert of mind and brimming with genius, he was good in everything that interested him, and rotten in everything that didn't.

He made almost every team in school, except the Glee Club. He was at once the most careless, the most amusing, the most genial, the most warm-hearted, understanding boy in school. We called him "Rube," but we voted him the best all-round man in his class.

Languages were always his downfall. He was so bad in German that his irate teacher shied the inkwell at him, and in college he flunked French so repeatedly and convincingly that he failed to graduate.

7

But English was his heart's desire. He pored over the poets, the novelists, historians and short story writers. He took his drama direct from the stage in Boston, specializing, as I remember it, in a course by Marie Doro on *The Morals of Marcus Ordeyne.* I hope Mr. Kieran will correct me if that is not the subject she was giving.

What work he did in other courses was swiftly, often brilliantly done in the last moments before each assignment was due. I dimly recall one other thing besides foreign languages that did not interest Heywood, and that was packing. The technique he employed was fascinating to everyone except his roommate. It consisted in throwing everything in sight into the trunk until it ran over, and then he climbed in himself and trampled it all down.

Heywood was in a ferment in college; his genius was boiling, but it would not jell. The big, genial boy, to whom it had been easy to be "tops" at school, was finding the outside world less flexible. How he crystallized his ability at last through his humor, his genius and fighting spirit is shown in the number of his admirers here tonight and in the caliber of the other speakers who have come to do him honor.

So that I might not rank myself with these Olympians behind me, I was told by my daughter, when she read the list of speakers, "Why, Daddy, you're the only one in the whole lot that I never heard of before!"

Heywood Broun became a newspaperman in 1910 when he joined the staff of the New York MORNING TELEGRAPH. *He was fired two years later on the occasion of his second request for a raise. During the next nine years he was, in order, reporter, rewrite man, copyreader, Sunday magazine editor, dramatic critic, book reviewer and columnist. In 1917 he married Ruth Hale, novelist and head of the Lucy Stone League, who died shortly after a friendly divorce in 1934. They had one son, Heywood Hale Broun.*

As a war correspondent in France in 1917 and 1918 Broun wore a uniform so badly that General Pershing asked him if he had fallen down. His pen was facile on any subject and his baseball stories, in the TRIBUNE *and later the* WORLD, *have been rated among the best ever written.*

L ADIES AND GENTLEMEN: This [indicating paper] isn't my speech, it's just a rollcall of the meeting. I was warned to speak on Heywood Broun and not on politics. I'll keep it clean.

John Kieran

Heywood was a great baseball fan, as many of you know, and one of his columns I recall very well, although written some twenty-odd years ago, was regarding two pitchers on the New York Giants. One was a pitcher by the name of Rube Schauer [pronounced Shower], who wasn't very good, and was frequently chased from the ground by the enemy bats, at which times he was relieved by a left-hander named Ferdy Schupp. So Heywood finally evolved a line, after seeing a good many of these duets, that "it never Schauers but it Schupps."

It is just little things like that that stick in your mind. Of course, he wrote a great many leading lines that lightened the columns of the *World* and the *Telegraph,* that stayed in our minds at the time, but just coming here tonight and seeing this crowd of persons here reminds me of something different. It reminds me, if you will let me go a little roughneck for a minute, of three words from Horace, *"Non omnis moriar,"* and that was written about two thousand years ago by another writer, like Heywood. I mean he was a writer and a good one, which Heywood was. He said, "I shall not altogether die," and in looking at this vast crowd sitting down here to bear testimony of their affection and esteem for a writer, I think that Heywood, too, could have written with Horace, *"Non omnis moriar."*

In 1921, Broun joined the WORLD. *His column, "It Seems to Me," matured from genial nature studies to serious political discussion. He began then to reveal the social consciousness which so often moved him to crusades endearing him to the under-privileged, but enraging his employers. The column appeared in the famous, now lamented* WORLD *with Rollin Kirby, Deems Taylor, Frank Sullivan, F. P. A. and Laurence Stallings.*

YES, Laurence Stallings and many others, and especially Alison Smith. Miss Smith, Alex Woollcott's assistant, was in one cell together with the desk of Broun. The drama was represented by Deems Taylor and Quinn Martin, who was the motion picture editor.

Franklin P. Adams   I had a contiguous cubbyhole, but it was lonely in there and I spent most of my time in the main curio or "hellzapoppin'" room. The Broun desk was usually buried under a recurrent flow of unanswered, often unopened letters. I doubt, after the first year, whether he ever used his typewriter. He would use anybody else's or write his stuff at home and bring it in, or send it in.

There's something about that Sacco-Vanzetti stuff that should be told. Those were the days when the *World,* alas, had its first edition on the street about 9:30, maybe earlier. Is that right, Mr. Swope? Mr. Kieran, I know you will correct me, if I am wrong.

Well, there was a request for copy from one of the departments, that it should get in early. Sunday was a short-handed day. It was August and the so-called Executive Editor was at Saratoga Springs. Mr. W. P. Beazell was in charge.

Six, seven, eight o'clock and no Broun column for Monday. Broun and I, as antiquarians will recall, divided three columns, a column-and-a-half measure each. So Mr. Beazell, desperate, had some other stuff to plug the hole. At nine, the Broun stuff arrived. It was too late to set the first edition, so Beazell carried it over. I still think that Beazell should have run the second edition, then there wouldn't have been any fight about that thing at all for quite a while.

The next day, Broun was sore. No editor but Swope seemed to know that you had to give Broun utter freedom and he would stay forever happy. Imply that he had better lay off this or that, and he would rebel. He hated the show of authority more than he hated authority. So they patched up a column in Broun's space when it was nine o'clock, and no Broun copy in.

The truth of the matter was that Broun was spending the week end in Long Island. He said he wrote the column some time that Sunday, in ten minutes during the afternoon, and then he said, "I'll have to go in to the *World* and take my stuff in."

Somebody else said, "Don't bother about it. I'm going in by car, and I'll take it in."

Broun said, "All right."

So the man took it in, in the car, and went home for dinner and sent his chauffeur down to the *World* building. The chauffeur went out to dinner. This was for Monday's paper, Monday morning's paper, so he probably thought any time Monday was time enough, and he came down there about half-past nine. That is the reason why that stuff didn't get printed the first day. The rest of the story is that where Mr. Broun spent the week end was at the home of Mr. Otto Kahn.

HEYWOOD did me a thousand favors during our friendship, but I can remember at least one occasion when I was of service to him. He and Connie came to Saratoga for a few days' amusement at the

Frank
Sullivan

tracks and at the roulette wheel. Heywood hadn't been doing so well at the roulette wheel, so Connie suggested that he give up going around to the hot spots at night and just have himself a little fun at the track in the early afternoon.

Well, that was something that Heywood had to get around. That afternoon he and I happened to meet, and Heywood asked me how I was, and I said I felt all right except that I had a little cold. That gave him an idea.

After dinner that night, when they were supposed to stay home and play bridge, he told Connie that he had heard that I was seriously ill with laryngitis and he said, "Don't you think I ought to go over and see Frank and see how he is?" And Connie said, "Of course, by all means do that." So Heywood went out to Saratoga Lake and went ahead and played the wheel until morning. When the next night came around, it seemed that I had about a dozen more diseases, and Heywood had to come over and sit with me again. If I had had all the diseases that Heywood thought up for me on those two nights, the Harvard Medical Museum would have been bidding for me.

However, he made the mistake of not letting me in on it. Everything would have been all right if he had tipped me off, but he didn't. The next day, I happened to go out to the race track, which I didn't do every day, and I ran into Connie, and to her I seemed to look in the pink of condition. There were a few explanations demanded and I didn't know the answers, so that was the end of Heywood's roulette for that week. That was really the only favor that I ever did for him, if it was a favor.

13

In 1927, a fish peddler and a shoemaker, one named Sacco, the other Vanzetti, were legally executed by the State of Massachusetts on the crest of a wave of witch-hunting hysteria which outraged all who knew the facts. Broun poured his devastating writing talent into two columns, attacking the holiest of holy reaction so sharply that his editors requested him to write no more on the subject. He went on a one-man strike and refused to write more for the WORLD *until it would print two more columns which he had prepared. Herbert Bayard Swope, then the executive editor, persuaded him to return.*

GUESTS and Fellow Newspapermen, for I am one at heart and always shall be. I may have been Heywood's boss, but he was my benefactor. I shone in his reflected glory. I made him a columnist, in spite of his doubts, and with him I worked out that *Herbert Bayard* gentle, misleadingly moderate head, "It Seems to *Swope* Me," which the column carried for almost nine years in the *World,* from 1921 to 1929, and which he used until the end a few days ago.

Paraphrasing a now celebrated quotation, Heywood was a gin-drinking, poker-playing, wicked old reprobate. But the other side of his shield was filled to overflowing with his virtues. I think we loved him as much for his delightful frailties as we did for the qualities that made him a marked man.

All eulogies are written in terms of the author. He will unconsciously attribute to his subject the qualities he likes to see in himself. You will perceive, then, that I am chiseling on him in the story I will now tell.

14

Last summer, Heywood was awarded a distinguished newspaper prize by the Headliners Club. In receiving it, he replied, after a curious premonition which caused him to say this, that he thought it would be his last year in journalism. He said: "In signing off, I would like to ask a blessing on all whose fingers, hearts and souls are sprayed with the fine badge of ink. It may be that newspapers which die in a state of grace go to heaven, and if my luck holds and the time comes, St. Peter will say to me, 'Heywood, here's your old job back on the old *Morning World.*' And that would be Heaven."

Can even so able and pituitary a labor leader as John Llewellyn Lewis ask for a better recommendation for a mere boss and for a newspaper?

Heywood's friendship was a privilege. I find myself wishing that the Great Gamekeeper could have spared him, in Heywood's familiar words, for "just a few more rounds."

Broun's columns on Sacco and Vanzetti belong to history along with the cause they espoused. His return to the WORLD *was brief, for he told off his publishers in another column printed in* THE NATION *on May 4, 1928. As a result, he was fired. He chafed at the futility, but never regretted his contribution to the martyrdom of Sacco and Vanzetti, to whose cause others had contributed energy, and some their fortunes.*

ABOVE any man I have known, Heywood Broun could say, and really mean it, when talking of Sacco and Vanzetti, or any victim of man's cruelty to man, "There, but for the grace of God, go I."

Gardner
Jackson

This strong humility, this feeling of himself in the shoes of the fellow in trouble, was a large factor in his burning lust for justice. He despised position and power for its own sake. His soul poured out eloquently in protest at the abuse of such position and power.

The combination of a Lowell of Harvard, a prominent Judge Grant of the Beacon Hill dinner tables, a Massachusetts governor, ordering the merciless execution of two Italians whom the facts proclaimed guiltless, fired Broun to crusade as he had never crusaded before.

Right after the electrocution of the poor fish peddler and the good shoemaker, Broun attended a secret dinner at the Coffee Club here in New York, with noted judges, lawyers, editors and writers. The questions discussed were: "What next in the Sacco-Vanzetti case?" "What are the lessons from it?" Never will I forget his scathing brilliance in answer to a distinguished lawyer and judge, who seri-

16

ously asserted that Sacco and Vanzetti might have been saved if "the radicals of the world had not organized to protest against their impending doom."

"You would still be sitting smugly in your chambers or your offices, unaware of the unjust fate of two unknown Italians, but for the organized voice and actions of the world's radicals and liberals," Broun replied.

Never will I forget his passionate sarcasm at those who urged an open mind, and referring to one particular editorial writer, he remarked, "His mind is so open that the wind whistles through it and nothing sticks."

"What can you build," he went on, "with a mind which hasn't the guts to stay on any side of the fence, when self-aggrandizement beckons to the other?"

Nor will I forget his scorn at counsels of respectability for purposes of expediency. "The respectability of all you gentlemen," he said with quiet emphasis, "did not stop the respectability of a Harvard president from helping to throw the switch on two innocent men."

In the manner he talked, he wrote—wrote columns the *World* would not publish. His were words stirring people to think and to act, a quality of words sorely needed in today's world, where the public mind is rapidly becoming inflamed by the propaganda of warring nations, of a Dies Committee, of a Father Coughlin, by the propaganda of fear and hate. Broun told me at the Coffee Club dinner, and many other times later, that his Sacco-Vanzetti experience cast the die for him. It made him pitch in with his great heart, his able pen and his high intelligence irrevocably with labor, whether on a farm or in an office and factory. He saw labor as the only force

17

capable of gaining strength enough and of having a deep enough desire among the multitudes to preserve and extend the democratic processes in our country.

The crucial struggles ahead call for more Heywood Brouns.

Broun's readers of "It Seems to Me" were legion and he did no searching for a job. The TELEGRAM *immediately invited him to its staff, with expected increase in circulation. By this time his personal affairs were so complex that he leaned heavily upon his lawyer.*

Hᴇʏᴡᴏᴏᴅ BROUN was not a client of any one person. He was a client of everybody. For "client" really means one who listens, and Heywood listened to people in all walks of life. It took him only twenty minutes or a half hour to write his column because he lived it during the previous twenty-four hours.

Morris L. Ernst

He wrote his column with words that we remember, because Helen Baker, who is in the audience, when Heywood was very young, taught him to choose the right word.

It is not easy for me to talk about Heywood. It was forty-two years ago that I started to drink with him, and in the last twenty-five years, two or three nights a week I would have a snifter with the big boy.

I have seen Heywood during his low moments, and he had them. I have walked the streets with him when he was in doubt. We drank together when he had moments of insecurity, emotional ones. He was always looking for certainty, always looking for finality, always fighting the boss. But intellectually he had no doubts; he was secure.

When it became my privilege to fight for the Newspaper Guild against William Randolph Hearst and the Associated Press, in the Morris Watson case that tested the National Labor Relations Act, it can be said without fear of contradiction by anyone connected with

19

the cases that Burgess* didn't win, Watson didn't win, Ernst had nothing to do with the winning. It was Heywood, with his simple, forthright, decisive determination of strategy.

Heywood made fabulous sums of money and never had a nickel, but I used to go down to the breadlines with him two and three decades ago, and Heywood would put his hand into his pocket and hand out a twenty-dollar bill exactly the same as a dime.

I miss him, thousands of people in this community of ours will miss him, because Heywood fought not people but philosophies and theories and principles, because he wanted to make this a decent world for every human being. He could fight people and he could, at the same time, sit and drink with them while fighting.

It is my privilege to read just three paragraphs from a letter written by the President of the United States about "my friend, Heywood Broun":

"The cause of true liberalism which he served well and faithfully through great crises suffered irreparable loss in the passing of Heywood Broun. When he died, I said that no matter for whom he worked, he wore no man's collar.

"As I look back now on the rich and full life which he led, it seems to me he was always at his best when advocating a cause unpopular with the majority. He was a hard fighter but a fair adversary and cared not for personal consequences so truth and conscience were on his side.

"His deep compassion, his bitter and burning pity for the oppressed, always moved him to eloquent protest and courageous action in the face of baffled justice. In him the underprivileged always found a steadfast friend.

[Signed] "FRANKLIN D. ROOSEVELT."

* Louis Burgess, fired by Hearst for Guild activity.

Broun was not satisfied only to write about politics, laws and lawmakers. His nature impelled him to be in the vanguard of progress. He wanted to be in Congress. In 1930 he won a Socialist nomination for a congressional post. Ruth Hale managed his campaign. After he lost, he left practical politics to more experienced hands.

IF I WERE not the Mayor of the city, perhaps I would not have been invited to this platform, but I would have been up in the gallery with the rest of you.

Fiorello H. LaGuardia   Heywood Broun and I had one thing in common: he was fired from as many newspapers as I have been fired out of political parties.

We all miss him. Try as hard as I could, this to me is a memorial. I can't laugh tonight. A great friend is gone. There is a void. His place has not and will not be filled for some time to come. He was an outpost in the vanguard of progress. Party labels meant very little to him. It was the issues and the cause that interested him and about which he wrote so tellingly and so forcefully.

Heywood had a great genius for expression. He had unusual courage, and he always had a nice way of saying bad things about me. I recall one instance when a very prominent gentleman met me in Washington. He had always been interested in Broun, and he showed me an article in which Broun implied by innuendo that I wasn't sincere. Later when I spoke to Broun, he looked down at me and he said, "Oh, no, I didn't mean that! I didn't say you were a crook!"

Broun knew conditions; he was a student of conditions. And, of course, he always had an accurate source of information. He associated with more nice people than I ever met in the Social Register, but he never went social, if you get what I mean.

He was true Liberal. He was a real progressive. And this is interesting, as I had occasion to observe. The forces of reaction didn't hate Heywood Broun because he was a radical; they didn't dislike him because he was a liberal; but how they feared him because he was truthful!

I recall very vividly the campaign of 1930. For a while, Heywood thought he wanted to go to Congress. It would have been refreshing to have him there. He conducted a unique campaign. He was campaigning in the 17th Congressional and I was campaigning up in the 20th. We were helping each other. We were both on different tickets, but we had the same platform. Heywood would start out in the cool of the evening and he would make one or two speeches, and then he would have to cross a meeting of one of his opponents. Heywood would stop to listen and become interested in what his opponent was saying.

Well, he didn't get elected, but he subsequently became very active in Congressional affairs. And I can tell you that in those days, the stock-ticker-plus-carrying days, many of the conservative gentlemen of Congress would read Heywood Broun's column after they had read the quotations of the Stock Exchange. He was a telling force because he would criticize his own friends just as quickly and sincerely as he criticized his opponents. He was really and sincerely tolerant and could not stand the intolerance of a colleague.

It is refreshing that his work was so truly impressive that many thousands miss him now. In these times, when so many of us believe that there is much yet to be done, and many of us are seeking to improve conditions, we feel the need of his forceful and clear statements.

22

No one during Heywood Broun's career ever questioned his sincerity or for a moment doubted that he wasn't speaking right from the heart. He never followed editorial policy, he never curried favor with anyone—qualities that are sorely needed in the journalism of today.

I am just one of the thousands and thousands who miss him. I am one who profited very often by his sharp criticism. I am one who was helped by his sincere encouragement. It is fitting and proper that we meet today to pay tribute to his memory on the birthday of Abraham Lincoln. Heywood loved humanity as Abraham Lincoln loved humanity. A course at Harvard College did not spoil Heywood Broun.

A great leader, a true liberal, a useful journalist, a fine American!

Heywood Broun had readers in every field of thought or endeavor. Sports fans read him as an authority when he wrote about sports. He was an equal authority on subjects foreign or remote to sports fans. He was respected in the theater by patrons, producers, writers and actors.

IT WOULD be deeply satisfying to me to name all those qualities in Heywood Broun that the ever-fresh memory of him keeps vividly before my eyes. Listing his virtues as man and writer would be the pleasantest inventory I ever made.

Edward G. Robinson   With his great bulk, there was a spirit that was solid and delicate, giant-like and gentle. He was a gallant knight who smiled at his own gallantries and his own generosities. He was clear-eyed about himself and especially about his weaknesses. We all found strength in our own weaknesses because Heywood by his own protective charm showed us how to admit them and how to transform the meanness of them into something better.

Of course he was for the underdog, of course he crusaded against injustices, and of course he was a champion of lost causes. But that description of Heywood leaves so much of his greatness out. I'd be willing to give anything to be able to hear Heywood say the things about himself that I am groping to express. It would be an honest, playful exaggeration, and it would be an honest, playful belittling; but truth would pervade it all.

I want to speak of Heywood Broun as I remember him when I was a beginner, a novice in the acting profession. Heywood was the only one of the play reviewers who disregarded the snobbish, or maybe cautious, custom of the reviewers of the day—the separation between actor and critic. I am not too clear as to what he said about my acting in those early days, but I do remember the encouragement he gave to me and to many others, not only in his reviews, but in his non-patronizing talks with me.

I would go to his home—a transgression, I suppose, against the critic's code in those days—and talk, making fine aspirations of the theater a natural and simple thing, and making experimental and pioneer work in the theatre a natural and simple thing. No condescension! How could Heywood be condescending? No priggishness! How could Heywood be priggish? Just Heywood—simple, great and easily worshiped. He was too great to die, and as for me, he still lives.

Broun's interest in the theater went further than that of a writer looking for something to write about. He was a champion of the Federal Theater and himself pointed the way toward that wonderful project when, in order to give employment to actors, he produced and played in SHOOT THE WORKS. *The show was moderately successful, but Broun lost all he had and all he could borrow on the venture.*

THIS IS a rather trying ordeal for me, due to an inhibition caused by a remark of Broun's one time while I was expostulating and beating the table in an argument on the rich. He said to me, "Mac, it's a shame that with a voice like yours, you don't ever know what the hell you're talking about!"

Edward McNamara

It is also rather difficult for me to stand here and hear him eulogized so beautifully, when I knew the other side. He invited me to come and live with him in a house at 85th Street, and he said, "By all means bring your trunk." I was in the house only twenty-four hours when he received an invitation to meet the Duchess of Something or Other at a dinner at Mrs. Hearst's house on Riverside Drive.

He said to me, "I wonder if you, by any chance, have brought your tail coat and vest?" So I brought out the tail coat and vest and he tried them on. Those of you who knew his stature and mine can draw your own conclusions as to what he looked like. He put on my coat and vest, and then there was a space of about eight inches between the bottom of the vest and the top of the trousers.

I said to him, "You can't go like that. You can't do that!"

"Oh, yes, I can," he said. "I can put my thumb in the bottom of the vest and my pinkie in the top of the trousers and I will put them together. I can eat Marquis of Queensberry rules, one arm free!"

Well, he went to the party. Frank Adams was there and he could tell you from there on. I wouldn't know about that.*

But I do know about his coming home some time early in the morning. He leaned over in getting out of the cab and when he came in, a great piece of the fabric of the coat had let go. He came in, arguing about unions. "It's one thing you can say about the unions, anyhow. They'll find out that the seams are better than they make the fabrics."

Then I went to work in a picture uptown, in that theatre that burned up at 135th Street. Living with Broun at that time and making that picture, I came home one night at eight o'clock and found my trunk in the lobby, in the vestibule near the front door and a note to call him up at his new address. I went out to a phone and I called him up and I said, "What's the matter?"

"Oh," he said, "I forgot to tell you that I sold the house!" And I found myself and the trunk out on the sidewalk.

* Broun and I had been invited to a dinner at Mrs. Hearst's apartment, on Riverside Drive. The dinner was set for eight o'clock. Owing to the fact that it took me a long time to find my shirt studs, I didn't get there until 8:15, but I was the first one there. Second to arrive was Broun, bending from the waist. He told me that the coat and vest were McNamara's, but the pants were his. There was a hiatus between the bottom of the vest and the top of the pants, a great gap showing if he stood erect. So when the women—and pretty stylish they were, too—arrived, and Heywood was introduced, his bend was interpreted as an indication of old-world politeness. Mrs. Norman De R. Whitehouse told me that she couldn't understand where Broun got that reputation for being a great rude bumpkin.—F. P. A.

That and a great many more things they allow me two minutes to tell you, two minutes to tell you what I know about Broun and what he did to me. It's just upside down, because it would take you two hundred years to tell you what he could do to you in two minutes!

Broun liked to play poker. It is not strange; he lived one of the fullest lives on record. It may be an exaggeration that he called taxicabs to carry him across the street, but a legend of some authentication is that he sometimes kept a taxicab waiting as long as eight hours while he was deciding to quit a poker game.

THANK YOU for your encouragement!

Well, it's true that Mr. Broun never walked. He always rode in taxis. No matter how short the distance and no matter how short the call, he always gave the driver a quarter tip. Of course, the longer the calls, the larger the tip. I know, because I drove Mr. Broun seven or eight years, steady—and many a dollar tip I got from him!

Charles Horowitz

We taxi drivers, however, not only loved Mr. Broun for his liberal tips, but we loved him also for his liberal views and support.

Of all the fine qualities this prince of men had, I liked best his fine, grand sense of humor, because I was able to kid him, and he could take it. For instance, one day when he came out of his office in the *World-Telegram* building on West Street, where I always got him, he said: "We're going up to the Racquet and Tennis Club today, Charles."

I said, "Yes, Mr. Broun."

While going up there, I said, "Did you say the Racquet and Tennis Club, Mr. Broun?"

He said, "Yes, Charles."

I said, "You mean that institutional place on Park Avenue?"

29

He said, "Yes, I still belong to it, you know. Quite true, I haven't been there in some time. I hope they let me in."

Then, of course, there was the other time when he came out and said, "I'd like to go to the Gotham Hotel today, Charles."

I said, "Yes, Mr. Broun. You know, that's a fine hotel. Been up a long while, too. I can remember over twenty years ago picking up that famous pianist, Mr. Paderewski, for a fare."

He said, "I'm going up to see our good friend, Mr. Lewis, today."

"Oh, I see!" I said. So I waited until we got in front of the hotel and the doorman came to open the door, and I slipped out and said, "Let me shake your hand, Mr. Broun, please."

Mr. Broun looked at me, wondering what was coming off, and I said, "Thank you! Now I am shaking the hand that is going to shake the hand of our great, true leader, John L. Lewis!"

They tell me I have one minute more, so here I am, back again.

There was the time when we were going uptown, and Mr. Broun, for the first time, asked me for a cigarette. I said, "I'm sorry, Mr. Broun, I haven't got a cigarette," but I did offer him my Corona-Corona (five cents)! He accepted the cigar, and a couple of times I looked around to see if he was smoking it. Sure enough, he was!

When I brought him to his destination and he paid me off, I said, "Mr. Broun, you certainly are a swell guy! Think of you smoking a five-cent cigar, even though it might be killing you, to please a friend!"

Thank you!

On January 9, 1935, Broun married Connie Madison, who survives him. With her, during his later years, he spent much of his time enjoying a 100-acre farm in Stamford, Conn. His neighbors included Deems Taylor, Westbrook Pegler, Quentin Reynolds and Gene Tunney. With some of them he founded the CONNECTICUT NUTMEG, *later taking over its debts himself and continuing it as* BROUN'S NUTMEG, *for which he wrote a prodigious amount of copy under his own and many other names.*

BROUN was a man who never believed that you could defeat ideas by hating men. Broun never hated anyone in his life, and as far as I know, only two men living ever hated Broun, and I think that this meeting would not be complete without mention of their names. I mean William Randolph Hearst and Westbrook Pegler.

Quentin Reynolds

I don't know why Mr. Hearst hated him. Five years ago, Mr. Hearst offered him the greatest contract ever offered a newspaperman, with $25,000 bonus, but Broun thought it over. He went to a very good friend of his, strangely enough Arthur Brisbane, for advice. They talked it over and Brisbane wouldn't, for the longest time, advise him. They sat in Brisbane's study and above his desk was a picture of Brisbane's father, Albert Brisbane, who, in his day, had been a great liberal leader. Broun said, "What a magnificent head on your father!" And Brisbane said, "You know, Heywood, he never would have worked for Hearst!" And Heywood said, "That's my answer."

Why Peg hates Broun, I don't know. We were great friends,

31

Broun and Peg and Deems Taylor, all of us, up in the country. We played poker at Broun's house one night and Peg's the next week, and Peg was a genial and charming host. Then in a few weeks, a week before Broun died, Peg showed his hatred in a column in which, by implication, he called Broun a liar and directly said that he could be coupled with Stalin and Hitler as an apostle of insincerity.

Broun knew that Peg hated his ideas, but he had known that for twenty years, and had accepted it, just as he didn't like Peg's ideas. But it was the first time in his life, I think, that Broun's honesty and sincerity had ever been attacked.

I think that Broun, who is dead, will live a lot longer than little men who try to defeat ideas by hating their fellowmen.

Long before the American Newspaper Guild, Broun was
president of a union of reporters. Only a few remain who
remember that union. It collapsed.

YES, that reporters' union collapsed, and it wasn't the first. There
probably were others before that. There was one effort to form a
newspaper union in New York in 1918 and the men who were caught
trying to organize that union were fired.

Lewis   Broun knew all about that but it didn't faze him,
Gannett   although it kept most other working newspapermen
                 from coming to meetings. When we formed the New
York Presswriters' Union in 1921, most of us who came to the meet-
ings were safe. We worked for the *Nation* and the *New Republic*.

Broun didn't attend. He meant to, but just didn't get around to
meetings on time. He wasn't a very active labor agitator back in
1921, but we knew that he was the only man with a newspaper by-
line who dared let his name be used publicly for a newspaper union
at that time.

We called him on the telephone and asked him to be the president.
"Well," he said, "you know, I've got a contract with the *World,* and
I really don't think it would be right to break that contract and
go out on strike. But I'll be president if I don't have to go on strike
in violation of my contract."

Of course that union never got anywhere near a strike. It took
all its life and time to fight red tape and get itself established as a
federal union of the A. F. of L. It worked itself into that "collapse."

Then, in 1933, Heywood Broun called a group of us to his apartment, and the American Newspaper Guild was born. A year later,

33

someone remembered a surplus in the old Presswriters' Union treasury—a couple of hundred dollars, too—and it was turned over to the new Guild. Broun, when told about it, scratched his head and said, "Oh, yes, I remember! That was the union of which I was president, but I never went to a meeting of it."

Those were Heywood's apprenticeship days as union organizer.

Anyone visiting the Broun home in Stamford, or even temporary quarters in Manhattan, would find books in various stages of binding scattered from the kitchen table to the fish pond. They were likely to be candidates for the Book-of-the-Month Club choice, of which Broun was a judge. Some say he read all the books.

I REALLY haven't any right to be here, because most of the people who are talking tonight knew Heywood so much, so much better, really, than I did, if you can count knowing him better in terms of seeing him oftener.

Edna
Ferber

I met Heywood twenty-five years ago, in a saloon. In that day, they didn't call them night clubs or taverns; they called them saloons, and this was a little saloon behind the theatre in which the Washington Square Players started. (That is the Guild Theatre group now.)

I fell in love with Heywood in a perfectly nice way. I not only loved to listen to that extraordinarily beautiful speaking voice of his, but I loved to listen to what he had to say because it was so different and so courageous.

Twenty-five years ago, most people didn't say the things that Heywood was saying. They are all saying them now, but he said them first; at least, for me he said them first.

It seems to me that the things that Heywood had to say were so important that when I read them I felt that I wanted to write better than I had been writing; and when I heard them, I wanted to be better than I was. That may sound a little sentimental and silly, but it isn't, really. I not only wanted to write better than I had been writing, but I wanted to write better than I could; and I not only wanted to be better than I was, but I wanted to be better than I could be, and that is, I suppose, that little touch of God that Heywood had in him.

Broun was a union man from the heart. He picketed when picketing was necessary and he never questioned another workingman's picket line. When the waiters of one of his favorite night clubs considered a strike, one of them asked him for tactical advice. "Tell me who your favorite customer is," said Broun. "I'll write him a letter and tell him to stay away." The waiter replied, "Why, you are, Mr. Broun."

IT IS a great privilege to be here tonight, as Mr. Broun's favorite waiter, to pay tribute to the man who was beloved by everyone. The whole world acclaimed him as a liberal—to me he was a liberal—and a liberal tipper he was, too.

Karl Virag

The rates were much higher than Mr. Horowitz's and without the premium of giving away cigars.

Broun admired vigor and vigorous movements. As a union leader he was sometimes inclined to be impetuous. He knew that about himself, and never hesitated to ask the advice of more experienced leaders. Often as not the advice was "Keep your shirt on." This from John L. Lewis, for whom Broun had great affection.

HEYWOOD BROUN has joined that innumerable caravan that moves to that mysterious world where each shall take his place in the last call.

John L. Lewis   I think that most of us, as we near the total of our lives, feel increasingly that we have lost a friend, a great public figure, one in whom we knew we might have profound confidence.

I confess to a very great sense of loss in the passing of Heywood Broun. Many, many times during his late illness, he occupied my thoughts, and I suppose that in a subconscious way, I was trying to encourage him in the fight he was making. And yet, at the same time, it seemed to me to be a more or less settled fact that Heywood would not win that fight. Perhaps I can solace my own spirit in the thought that he was a weary, weary man, because, my friends, no one man, no one spirit, no matter how valiant or how great, can for a long time try to move the great mountains of indifference, self-complacency or self-satisfaction. The man who undertakes to move the world about in any direction or upon any surface must of necessity expect to spend a tremendous degree of energy, and if he continues that fight from his tender years, he will finally find a diminution of his strength and that energy which he may have possessed in the beginning. It matters not that the man may be a genius like Heywood Broun, because

38

strangely adverse winds may blow and cause the spark of genius to flutter and flutter like a candle in the wind, and some day lose its fire.

On the other hand, at times Heywood Broun was broody and discouraged. Often his ideas were hurled back upon him, and great numbers of the people throughout the land undertook to assail his philosophy and to deny the premise of his writings. I can understand how at times he sought to hide his bruises beneath a kindly humor, behind the eccentricities of his strong and powerful personality, and yet, though a young man, he grew ill, and I doubt if, in his final illness, it was not easier for Heywood Broun to depart, rather than remain with us.

I think that this country of ours and every man and woman in it are better off because Heywood Broun lived, because he had the temerity and the strength to tear aside that veil of deceit and hypocrisy which sometimes obscure public vision on a public question.

No matter how severe or how great the strain, I think that if the people of our country are to continue their lives in more than orderly fashion, then we certainly need, in order to understand the hopes and aspirations of our life, more men like Heywood Broun in our national life, to whom God had given special talents and to whom we owe a great debt. But perhaps it is well that not everyone possesses the great talents and outstanding courage and strength, for they might utilize those talents in their pursuit for the acquisition of money.

Money meant nothing to Heywood Broun except something that he might give away to alleviate the distress of some less fortunate individual. He was careless of his own concerns, he was careless of his mode of living, and he was careless of tomorrow, because if it became necessary, he could do without all of the ordinary things of life. So he devoted his life and his time and his genius to making a contribution toward the promotion of a better public understanding of public questions, never failing to come to the defense and rescue of the people.

Behind him, there were others, and in the privacy of our homes here in New York and in Heywood Broun's home, we came to an understanding that resulted in the organization of the American Newspaper Guild, of which he was the first president. It was a great national organization of the highly skilled workers in the writing profession, and I believe that to have been a remarkable contribution, not alone in a public sense, but in the sense of making a contribution to the writing and journalistic field, to the men and women in that field, in America.

Heywood Broun, in this fashion, made his own contribution, but he was also one of the great captains in America's modern labor movement. I am proud to take this moment here and now to say that I am glad to have been one of his official associates and co-workers, and I am glad that I have been able to call Heywood Broun my friend.

On August 7, 1933, when newspapermen were growing conscious of the meaning of unemployment, and resenting reduced pay checks, Broun printed a letter from an unemployed newspaperman in his column. The letter said: "The men who make up the papers of this country would never look upon themselves as what they really are—hacks and white-collar slaves. Any attempt to unionize leg, rewrite, desk or make-up men would be laughed to death by these editorial hacks themselves. Union? Why, that's all right for 'dopes' like printers, not for smart guys like newspapermen." The challenge stirred Broun, and what he wrote that day was the conscious genesis of what has been called his enduring monument—The American Newspaper Guild. He said:

"After some four or five years of holding down the easiest job in the world, I hate to see other newspapermen working too hard. It makes me feel self-conscious. It embarrasses me even more to think of newspapermen who are not working at all. Among this number are some of the best. I am not disposed to talk myself right out of a job, but if my boss does not know that he could get any one of forty or fifty men to pound out paragraphs at least as zippy and stimulating as these, then he is far less sagacious than I have occasionally assumed.

"Fortunately, columnists do not get fired frequently. It has something to do with a certain inertia in most executives. They fall readily into the convenient conception that columnists are something like the weather. There they are, and nobody can do much about it. Of course, the editor keeps hoping that some day it will be fair and warmer,

*with brisk northerly gales. It never is, but the editor re-
mains indulgent. And nothing happens to the columnist,
at least, not up to now.*

*"It is a little difficult for me, in spite of my radical lean-
ings and training and yearnings, to accept wholeheartedly
the conception of the boss and his wage slaves. All my very
many bosses have editors, and not a single Legree in the
lot. Concerning every one of them, it was possible to say,
'Oh, well, after all, he used to be a newspaperman once
himself.'*

*"But the fact that newspaper editors and owners are
genial folk should hardly stand in the way of the organization of a newspaper writers' union. There should be one.
Beginning at nine o'clock on the morning of October 1,
I am going to do the best I can to help in getting one up. I
think I could die happy on the opening day of the general
strike if I had the privilege of watching Walter Lippmann
heave half a brick through a* TRIBUNE *window at a non-
union operative who had been called in to write the current
'Today and Tomorrow' column on the gold standard."*

WALTER LIPPMANN has not heaved that brick. None of us
will live to see him do it. He is on the other side. We are more
likely to see Ogden Reid do it.

*Carl
Randau*

Heywood early recognized the simple truth about
building a union, that the toughest men are not always
among the bosses. They are often among those who
ought to be at our side.

Heywood had this discovery in mind one day when he was asked

42

why he gave so much time, so much money, so much energy to the Guild when there was nothing he could get in return.

"That is not correct," said Broun. "No matter how much I give to the Guild, I will always remain indebted to the Guild. It has been my education. The Guild did for me what Harvard couldn't do."

We all know that Heywood was the most gracious of men, a genuine diplomat. I watched him one day make a friend. It was after a particularly harassing conference with a publisher who fought the Guild at every point.

"You, Mr. X," said Broun, "are becoming my favorite publisher. None of this hypocrisy, none of this lip service to unions, with a whole basket of buts thrown in. You're just plain against us, just openly against unions, against your own employees." And then they went and bought each other a drink.

The job that Heywood started with that publisher and with all other publishers remains to be completed. Heywood told us he was enlisted for the duration. He made good on that promise. He was fighting for our rights at the very end. He stayed for the duration. I hope the same can be said of the rest of us, that we all are in for the duration.

Broun took the Newspaper Guild seriously. He fought hard, whether on the economic front or on the legal front. Sometimes he swept attorneys aside and barged in where they feared to tread. He argued with a United States Supreme Court justice about a Guild case. He told a federal district judge, in court, what he thought, though such telling was not in keeping with the court's own notions of dignity. He was never afraid to test the laws affecting labor, especially when those laws came from the courts rather than from the representatives of the people.

No, HEYWOOD was not afraid to test judge-made law. When the first labor injunction hit the Guild in the Newark *Ledger* strike in 1934, a drastic injunction was issued which prevented the use of the radio and prevented the Guild members from using their own *Guild Reporter*. Heywood Broun went at once to Newark, on a cold winter night, to test the Guild's constitutional rights on the *Ledger* picket line.

A. J. Isserman

He also was an aid in court in that injunction case. You might well imagine that Broun added great weight to the argument. He found, however, that as long as he had counsel, he couldn't speak himself, so after the legal argument was over, I was canned on the spot.

Broun then took up the task of answering the serious charges that were made against him. The first charge was that in his column he had described a certain non-striker, named Jack Boyle, as a trained seal, and thus intimidated Boyle. Broun explained very carefully to the judge that he hadn't done anything of the kind. He said that he

44

wrote in his column that he had taken a walk in Central Park and there, after watching the seals play, he had simply christened one of the seals, Jack Boyle. Broun argued that that was not intimidation. He said it was only mockery.

But there was a more serious charge of intimidation. He was charged with intimidating another non-striker, one Walter Wynn. Broun testified that he saw that non-striker in front of the picket line, and then in a most unusual fashion, very *unusual* for Broun, he lured that striker to Giddy's bar, which was just across the street. He said that he spent three hours in that bar. There was round after round of intimidation.

And as for violence, there was blow after blow in his argument and a punch in his logic. At the end, Broun said, "Do you see that white line which stretches across Giddy's dance floor? The Guild members who are on strike are on one side of that line, and you, Wynn, are on the other side, on the side of the employer. Why don't you make up your mind and decide what side of the line you will stay on, and come out and join the strikers?"

That intimidation was most unfair. By that time, after those three hours, Wynn was so confused that his vision was obscured as was his economic outlook. He couldn't see the white line at all, and shortly thereafter, intimidated to the gills, he left the bar to make his injunction affidavit.

Now, Heywood never forgot that white line while he was alive. I am sure that his spirit goes on in the hearts and minds of trade union men and others who believe in the extension of the good life. That spirit will always be on the workers' side of that white line that stretched across the floor of Giddy's dance hall.

45

We have a letter from a priest who lives far away and could not be here. He is Father Edward Dowling, S. J., a Guildsman. He writes:

"About a year ago this time Heywood stopped in St. Louis and we had a long talk. For the five or six hours he talked over his desire to become a Catholic. This was the first I knew of it. The one adamant point upon which he felt he could not yield an inch was his devotion to the labor movement. As he mentioned later in a column, he saw that there was no conflict but rather basic harmony between his labor views and the labor views of the Catholic Church.

"I think Heywood wanted to resign the heavy duties of the Guild presidency at Toronto (1937) and St. Louis (1938) but after his religious step he definitely wanted to be elected president at San Francisco (1939), lest resignation be misconstrued as a desertion of those labor principles for which he lived these last few years and for which, it may well be, he died.

"If I had been able to appear at the meeting I believe I would have closed my talk by applying to Heywood the last words of the last editorial of the New York WORLD. *They are:*

" 'Farewell!

" 'Let the last words of the WORLD *be those of Mr. Valiant-For-Truth in* THE PILGRIM'S PROGRESS:

" ' "My sword I give to him that shall succeed me in my pilgrimage, and my courage and skill to him that can get it." ' "

*Broun had no use for one-man movements. In the Guild
he encouraged the development of leadership. He watched
the organization survive what seemed to be overwhelming
counter-forces, and he was happy at the end to know that
what he founded and nurtured would endure without him.
Mr. Kenneth Crawford of Washington was elected to succeed him, not to fill the shoes that could never be filled,
but to carry on the tradition of democracy which Broun
made a passion during his six years of the presidency.*

H EYWOOD BROUN'S death was an irreparable loss to the Guild,
but we are trying to carry on.

I have just come from Chicago, where a strike against the Hearst
newspaper, the one that remains, is in its fourteenth
Kenneth G. month. That strike is still going strong in the face of
Crawford injunctions, thugs, and everything the management
can draw on. It is going to go on until we win it.*

One very hot night, several years ago, when the Guild was trying
to decide whether to follow Heywood Broun into the C.I.O., he came
to Washington to try to persuade us, persuade us not only to affiliate
with the C.I.O., but to accept the consequences of such an affiliation
and take in all newspaper workers not already organized. He spoke
earnestly and at length, but when the vote was taken, he had lost. The
Washington Guild wanted the C.I.O. affiliation but a union confined
to editorial workers.

President Broun was disappointed and not a little discouraged.
The debate went on informally after the formal meeting. The late

* The strike was settled successfully for the Guild on April 26, 1940.—Ed.

Paul Y. Anderson, the late Rodney Dutcher, Bob Allen and others traded arguments with Heywood. There were angry words, and finally Heywood stalked out of the meeting, thoroughly irked. Once his back was turned, the meeting became a testimonial to Broun. It was decided to send him a telegram of explanation. The next day, we received a reply. It said merely, "It was a hot night, wasn't it?"

Heywood was that kind of union leader. He led us by persuasion and, if we sometimes balked, it had been a hot night and we would take it up again some cooler day.

As everyone now knows, Heywood Broun got his way about industrial unionism, as he did about most things, and there are few, in the light of experience, who will question the soundness of his basic policies. The Guild will remain essentially what he made it—a democratic, militant trade union of newspaper workers, a union determined that the history of exploitation in the newspaper industry shall not repeat itself, a union taking its place and accepting its responsibilities in the labor movement. And we of the Guild think of it as something else, too. We think of it as Heywood Broun's living monument. We shall build it solid and high. The Guild must and will be a lasting monument to the memory of its founder.

On the morning of last December 18th, Broun's great heart was stopped by pneumonia. The day before he became ill he joined the staff of the New York POST, *writing but one column, which appeared on December 14th. The life of a great journalist, a great labor leader, genuinely beloved of millions, came to a close. His vibrant life left a vibrant memory, and a tradition which shall live as long as men struggle for betterment.*